Collins

Revised Edition

Vision 6

A Course on Values and Life Skills

Main menu
Learning objects
Search book or online
Page jump
Mark-up data
View fullscreen
Help menu
Bookmark page
Open tool panel
Insert note
Pen & highlight
Single/double page
Zoom in
Zoom out
Zoom 100%
Sound on/off
Record audio
Spotlight
Clear data
Interactive whiteboard mode
Collins DIGISUITE
Search here
Online Search
Page 14-15 / 24
All Pages
Table of Contents
Animation
Audio
Interactivities
Teacher's Resource
Learning Tools
Test Generator
Dictionary
IWB
READING
Read this poem and see what a sister does to take care of her little brother.
Little, helpless baby dear,
While within your cot you lie,
Sister is sitting near
She will sing your lullaby.
When at last you fall asleep,
Not the slightest noise she'll make;
Quiet as a mouse she'll keep,
Without letting her darling wake.
helpless: unable to take care of yourself
cot: a small bed with high sides for a baby
lullaby: a soft gentle song sung to make a child go to sleep
slightest: very small
quiet: making no noise
darling: a person who is loved very much by somebody
wake: to stop sleeping
26
COMPREHENSION
A. Choose the correct option.
1. The baby's sister is sitting
a. near the baby.
b. far from the baby.
c. in another room.
2. The baby's sister will
a. sing a lullaby.
b. play with the baby.
c. wake up the baby.
B. Answer the questions.
1. Where is the baby lying?
2. Who will keep quiet like a mouse?
3. How is the baby's sister? Think of and write two words to describe her.
Life Skills and Values
Caring for one's family
1. Imagine you are playing outside your house, and your little brother is sleeping inside alone. Suddenly you hear your brother cry. What would you do?
2. You are watching TV with your friend. Your sister is sleeping in the next room. Your friend asks you to raise the volume of the TV. What would you do?
27

Preface

Vision **Revised Edition**, a course on life skills and values, is an engaging value education series meant to enable learners lead a balanced, happy and successful life. The National Education Policy, 2020 proposes the revision and revamping of all aspects of the education structure to create a new system that is aligned with the aspirational goals of 21st century education, while building upon India's traditions and value systems. It also lays focus on critical life skills and values.

Vision Revised Edition follows an interactive and multidisciplinary approach and caters to all kinds of learners with different learning styles.

Values are presented through progressively graded stories, anecdotes or poems.

Life Skills as laid down by the World Health Organization (WHO) have been covered through interesting stories.

Each book contains special chapters and colourful spreads showcasing the **United Nations Sustainable Development Goals**, which are important to achieve a just and an equitable world for all.

21st Century Skills have been mapped to each chapter with the aim of creating well-rounded individuals thriving in a constantly changing world.

Mental health and well-being of young learners is of prime importance in today's world. Therefore, **Let's Do Yoga** poster has been introduced as a brand-new feature of the book. It contains simple and doable asanas with step-by-step guidance and illustrations.

The series also focuses on mindfulness and social-emotional learning through **'happiness activities'**. Young children learn by doing, hence the series has a variety of hands-on activities, encouraging quiet reflection and sound action.

Creating a safety net for children and making them aware of **child rights** is much needed in this age and time. *Vision* Revised Edition has special advice for children through which they can face situations in which they feel afraid, pressurized or unsafe.

Vision Revised Edition comes with **Collins DigiSuite** which offers digital content packed with animated stories, slideshows and interactive activities.

***Vision* Teacher's Manuals** offer comprehensive **Lesson Plans** and **Additional Worksheets** for teachers.

In This Series ...

Vision Revised Edition adheres to the National Education Policy, 2020. Features such as 21st Century Skills, Life Skills, multiple intelligences, Sustainable Development Goals and Let's Do Yoga all align with the new policy.

Discuss
Warm-up exercise familiarizes students to the mood of the chapter

Read along
A story or a poem based on a value

Figure out
Questions based on the chapter to ensure value inculcation

Project
Interesting projects based on the values taught

Relate
Application-based questions to check students' understanding

Happiness Activity
Interesting activities to promote 'happiness'

Act
Interesting activities that reinforce the value taught

Think and Say
Thinking questions that encourage students to think laterally

Remember
Brief pointers that the students can incorporate in their behaviour

Remember

- Plan your day in advance so that you complete all the tasks you want to do.
- Wake up and go to bed at fixed times.
- Ensure that you spend sufficient time on your duties, needs, family, friends and yourself.
- Stay focused so that you can allocate more time to the important things in life.
- Make full use of the time at your disposal. Remember, time once gone never comes back.
- Never forget that it is always the right time to help people.

Think and Say
You see a man shouting at a street child for cleaning his car without permission at a traffic crossing. What will you do?

Happiness Box

Enjoyable activities that promote 'happiness' and exercises based on multiple intelligences addressing different learning styles

- Musical
- Interpersonal
- Visual-Spatial
- Verbal linguistic
- Naturalistic
- Intrapersonal
- Logical Mathematical
- Bodily Kinesthetic

Child Rights and Empowerment

Useful, child-centric advice to create a safety net for children and make them aware of their rights

Sustainable Development Goals

Special chapter and a colourful spread showcasing the UN Sustainable Development Goals, a set of goals aimed at changing our world for better

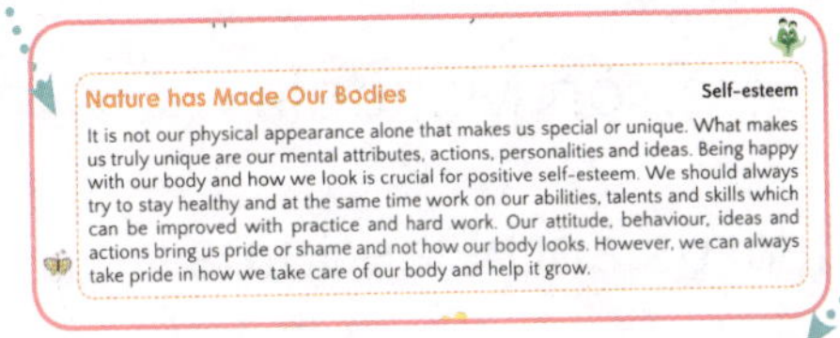

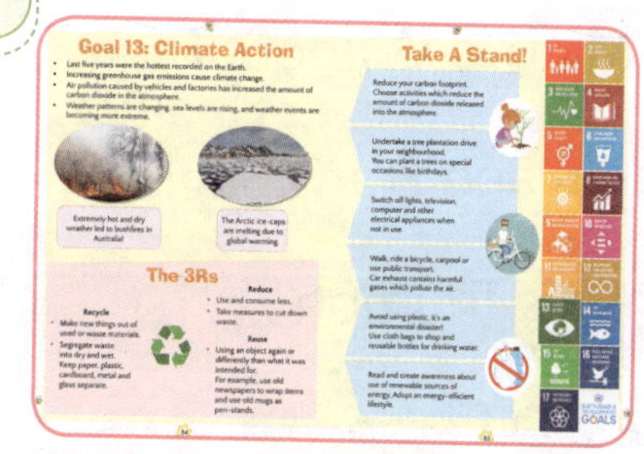

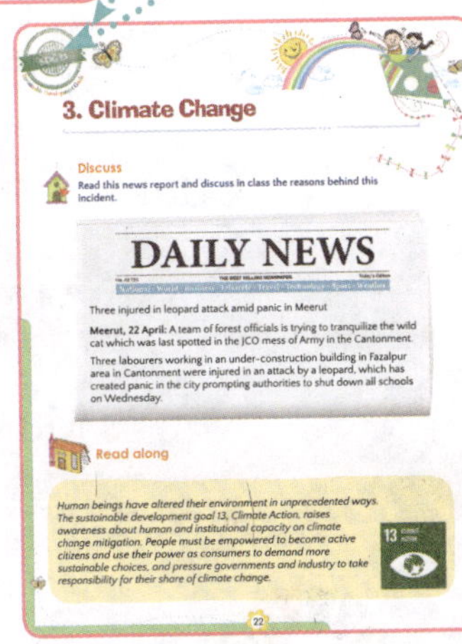

Poster

Colourful and interesting pull-out poster showcasing easy Yoga asanas

21st Century Skills

Skills necessary to succeed in the age of information: learning skills, literacy skills and social skills

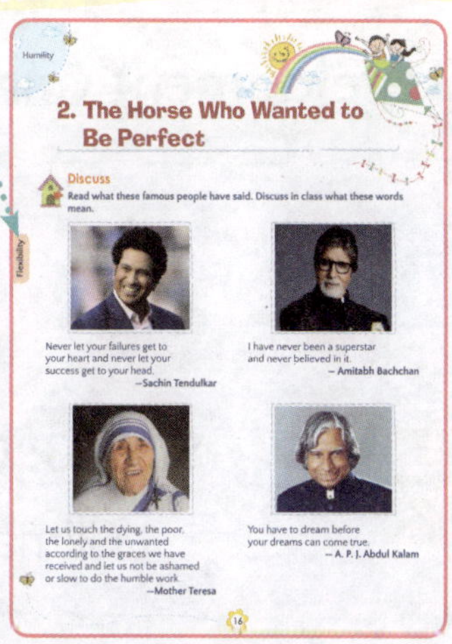

Life Skills

Chapters focusing on WHO life skills through interesting stories

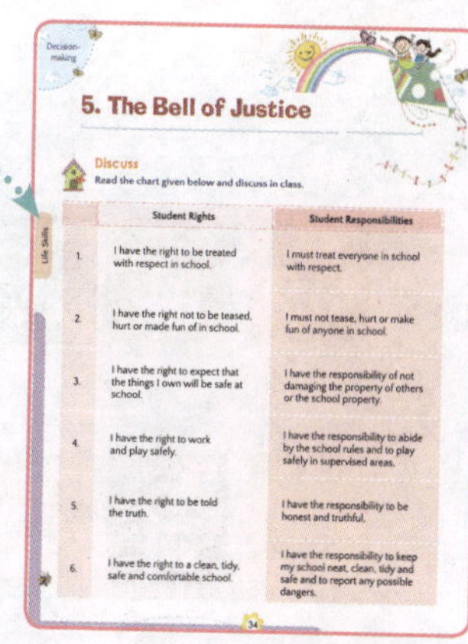

Teaching tips

- Explain how it is important to observe people's body language that tells us how they feel.
- It is important to be empathetic towards people without pretensions, else one will end up offending them.

Teaching tips

Suggestions for teachers

Detailed Contents

Values

Sustainable Development Goals

21st Century Skills

Learning Skills	Communication	A Trip to Venice
	Creativity	Icarus and Daedalus
	Collaboration	Mohun's Triumph
Literacy Skills	Cultural and Civic Literacy	Nelson Madela
Social Skills	Flexibility	The Horse Who Wanted to Be Perfect
	Tolerance and Objectivity	Gulliver's Adventures
	Citizenship	Where the Mind is Without Fear
	Ethical Behaviour	Charlie Brown and Franz Stigler
	Persistence	Make a Difference

Life Skills

The Bell of Justice	Decision-making
Eagle-Eyed Leon	Critical Thinking

Projects

Project I	Soda Bottle Greenhouse
Project II	The Lady with the Lamp
Project III	Greenhouse Effect
Project IV	Famous Personalities

Contents

1. A Trip to Venice

Discuss

Look at the pictures and discuss them in class.

A day from the life of the child, Mary Kom, the five-time World Amateur Boxing Champion.

Exercising and jogging at dawn.

Helping parents at home in the morning

Studying in the afternoon

Training for her sport in the evening

Read along

To: sunainat@gmail.com

CC:

Subject: Our trip to Venice

Hi Sunaina,

Good to know you are going to Venice for a vacation. We went there last year. On a holiday you can always pick and choose where you want to go or what you want to visit. That is what we did when we went to Venice. We were there for only four days. You had mentioned that you will be spending a whole week there. So you can do a lot more than what we did.

Still, let me describe to you how we spent our four days in Venice.

When we reached Venice at 8 am, we checked into the B&B Venice hotel. We chose this hotel as it is surrounded by the famous art galleries of Venice.

On our first day, we visited the galleries nearby as we were quite tired from our travel. We left at 9 am and could visit only four of them by 1.30 pm. I liked Ca' Pesaro the most. At 2 pm, we had lunch at Avogaria, a restaurant nearby. But don't visit it on Tuesdays. I noticed that it is closed on Tuesdays. After that, we enjoyed walking through the streets and alleys until night fell.

On the second day, we left at 8 am and had a quick breakfast at the pasticceria and proceeded to visit St. Mark's Basilica which opens at 9 am. You need a whole day to view it properly. We had packed our lunch and ate it sitting on a garden bench. Venice has very little night life, so we always headed back to the hotel once our sightseeing for the day was done.

On the third day, we left a bit late. We had planned to take the vaporetto for a Grand Canal Tour at 1 pm. At 11 am, we reached the French market cafe. The tables by the canal outside the cafe were so inviting that we sat there. My parents ordered a sumptuous brunch. I must tell you what happened while we were waiting for our order to arrive. Sitting on the next table was an elderly couple. Suddenly, the man started gasping for breath. He was nearest to me, and I wanted to help but I hesitated. I was not sure whether this was the right time and right place to approach total strangers. Perhaps they would not understand my English accent. But my father stood up instantly and quickly went to the man. I was surprised to see that my father did not wait to think whether it was the right time to help him or not.

The man was having an asthma attack. My father helped him inside the cafe. Thankfully, there was a doctor among the visitors. He gave the old man some medicine in an inhaler. Soon, the man was feeling better. Only after he was sitting upright and was breathing normally, we went back to our table. I looked at my father with admiration. I was so proud of him.

After we had finished eating, we took a tour of the Canal on Venice's water bus. It was great fun sailing on it.

That night, when I thought about the incident, I realized that there was no right time to help a fellow human. When another person needs help, one should extend it without hesitation. The moment of helping the person is the right time for that action. If one hesitates, the moment passes and one loses the opportunity, as I nearly did. It was my father who knew this truth. Because him, we were able to be humane to a person who needed our help. For, isn't it the duty of all human beings to be humane?

On the fourth day, we went to watch a glass-blowing demonstration on Murano Island. We had to take a boat which left quite early. So we left our hotel at 6 am. The hotel staff, very kindly, packed our breakfast to take with us.

Visiting this island is a must. It's the easiest one to visit, but again it will take up a whole day.

Since you will have more time than we had, you can try hiking on Torcello Island and also indulge in some window shopping at the Rialto Market. Unfortunately, we had no time for that. Have loads of fun and mail me photos of your holiday.

Please convey my regards to your mother and father. Your dear friend,

Supriya

Think and Say

You have to study for an important exam. Your friend wants you to play a cricket match that evening. How will you do both the activities?

Remember

- Plan your day in advance so that you complete all the tasks you want to do.
- Wake up and go to bed at fixed times.
- Ensure that you spend sufficient time on your duties, needs, family, friends and yourself.
- Stay focused so that you can allocate more time to the important things in life.
- Make full use of the time at your disposal. Remember, time once gone never comes back.
- Never forget that it is always the right time to help people.

Figure out

A. Tick the correct answers.

1. Why did Supriya email Sunaina the itinerary?
   a. Supriya wanted to help Sunaina plan her own trip. ☐
   b. Supriya wanted to show off her trip to Venice. ☐
2. Why did Supriya mention that the Avogaria was closed on Tuesdays?
   a. She wanted to give Sunaina's family information unavailable to first-time tourists. ☐
   b. She wanted to boast that she knew more about Venice than Sunaina. ☐

3. Why did Supriya hesitate to help the sick, elderly man?
   a. She was indifferent to his condition.
   b. She was unsure if it was the right time to help a stranger.

4. Why did Supriya admire her father?
   a. Supriya admired her father because he was very knowledgeable.
   b. Supriya admired her father because he helped a stranger.

5. Apart from enjoying her trip, what will always remind Supriya of Venice?
   a. The many souvenirs she brought from Venice.
   b. The lesson that it is always the right time to help people.

B. Elucidate the saying, 'When somebody needs help, we should extend a helping hand immediately, for that is the right moment to take action.'

Relate

Tick the best options for these situations.

1. Your father asks you to buy some flour from the shop for a cake he is going to bake but you want to watch a show on the TV. What will you do?
   a. tell your father you would get the flour in the evening
   b. manage time so that you get the flour and also watch the show
2. You attend a music class and then learn karate for an hour. Your mother wants you to also learn painting but that would leave you with no time for yourself. What will you do?
   a. make a timetable and try to attend all the classes and yet take time out for yourself
   b. try to make your mother understand that you need time for yourself
3. Your younger brother is sick and wants you to play ludo with him but you want to play outdoors with your friends. What will you do?
   a. neglect your brother and go out to play with your friends
   b. play with your brother to let him know that you care

4. Every evening before dinner, you have about half an hour when you don't have any work. What will you do?
   a. spend it with your family ☐
   b. browse the TV channels or play a game on your mobile ☐

Act

Managing Distractors

Often, we try to do two things at the same time such as doing homework while watching TV. The time we take to do the homework increases because we are distracted. If we can avoid distracters, we can manage our time well.

Here are some tips to manage distracters:

1. Try to sit in a place where you can focus on your studies.
2. Mute your phone while studying. Call back if its really important.
3. If you need to browse the Internet for your studies, stick to the questions you need answers to.
4. Avoid switching on the television while studying.
5. Take a break when you feel tired. Go for a walk or do something that refreshes your mind.

Happiness Box

1. **Good time management can be practised by inculcating some good habits. Read the instructions and fill in the table.**
   1. Write all the things that stop you from managing time effectively in the left column.
   2. Discuss possible ways of overcoming or avoiding this problem. Add the ways that you think will help you solve the problem in the right column.
   3. Share your problems and possible ways to solve them with your classmates. If you see ideas you think might work for you, add them to the table.
   4. Put up the table in your room.

What do I need to change?	How could I do things differently?

2. **Tick the activities you think are very important (VI), just important (I) or not important (NI) in your life.**

	Activity	VI	I	NI
1.	Watching a film	☐	☐	☐
2.	Eating a meal	☐	☐	☐
3.	Going for a picnic	☐	☐	☐
4.	Tidying up one's room	☐	☐	☐
5.	Singing a song	☐	☐	☐
6.	Helping parents	☐	☐	☐
7.	Taking a nap	☐	☐	☐
8.	Cheering up a sad friend	☐	☐	☐
9.	Baking a cake	☐	☐	☐
10.	Going to school	☐	☐	☐

Teaching tips

- Reiterate that there is no time like the present to help people, even if they are strangers.
- Stress on the fact that we have to clearly divide activities in our life into important and not important. We must slot more time for the important things and lesser time for the unimportant things of life.
- We must inculcate good habits so as to use time appropriately and avoid distractors.

2. The Horse Who Wanted to Be Perfect

Discuss

Read what these famous people have said. Discuss in class what these words mean.

Never let your failures get to your heart and never let your success get to your head.

—Sachin Tendulkar

I have never been a superstar and never believed in it.

— Amitabh Bachchan

Let us touch the dying, the poor, the lonely and the unwanted according to the graces we have received and let us not be ashamed or slow to do the humble work.

—Mother Teresa

You have to dream before your dreams can come true.

— A. P. J. Abdul Kalam

Read along

Once upon a time, there was a horse who nurtured a secret wish. The horse was beautiful and also had many good qualities. But it wanted to be perfect in every way. It especially wanted to be beauty unparalleled.

One day, the horse said to the Creator, 'O Lord, you have given me beauty and other good qualities, too. I am very grateful to you. But how I wish you could make me more perfect to look at. I would be extremely, extremely grateful if you could make me even more beautiful'.

The Creator said, 'I am more than ready to make you more beautiful. Tell me in what way you want to be changed'.

The horse said, 'It seems to me that I am not well proportioned. My neck is too short. If you can make my neck a little longer, my upper body will be infinitely more graceful. And if you can make my legs much longer and thinner, then I will look infinitely more elegant in my lower body'.

Think and Say

In a football match, you and your best friend are in opposing teams. Your team wins. Though your friend played well, his team lost. Everyone congratulates you, but ignores your friend, who you think is a better player. What will you do?

The Creator said, 'Amen'.

Immediately, a camel stood where the horse was standing. The horse was so disheartened that it started to cry, 'O Lord, I wanted to become more beautiful. In what way is this physical form more beautiful than my earlier form?'

The Creator said, 'Well, this is exactly what you had asked for. Long neck with thin, long legs are the features of a camel's body. You have become a camel now'.

The horse cried, 'Oh no, I do not want to become a camel. I wish to remain a horse. As a horse, everybody appreciated my good qualities. Nobody will appreciate me as a camel.'

The Creator explained, 'Never try to achieve or demand more than what I have given you. If you want to lead a life of desires and wishes, then every moment you will want more and more. You will always be dissatisfied. When your wishes are fulfilled, you will have no idea what the outcome could be. You demanded longer neck and legs and so I turned into a camel. Now you realize that you did not want to be a camel. Instead you prefer being a horse. Be happy as a horse and don't wish for more'. Saying this, the Creator turned the camel back into a horse.

The horse, now more enlightened, thanked the Creator. He was about to go on his way, when the Creator added, 'Remember that all things in my creation have their own good qualities. The camel is not as beautiful as you are, but it is a very useful creature. In the desert regions, human beings depend completely on the camel. A horse cannot be compared to a camel in those hot, sandy places. It carries heavy load, can walk long distances without water and has a tremendous sense of responsibility. Thus, each creature is valuable and must be respected as such.

Be humble and appreciate all life that exists in my creation.'

Nature has Made Our Bodies

Self-esteem

It is not our physical appearance alone that makes us special or unique. What makes us truly unique are our mental attributes, actions, personalities and ideas. Being happy with our body and how we look is crucial for positive self-esteem. We should always try to stay healthy and at the same time work on our abilities, talents and skills which can be improved with practice and hard work. Our attitude, behaviour, ideas and actions bring us pride or shame and not how our body looks. However, we can always take pride in how we take care of our body and help it grow.

Remember

- We can learn to value all life on the earth by being humble.
- Humility teaches us to listen more and say less.
- By being humble we can respect the opinion of others and earn their respect.
- By being humble, we can grow and improve.
- A humble life brings contentment, patience, forgiveness and compassion.

Figure out

A. Tick the correct answers.

1. The horse was beautiful and had many good qualities but he felt he was
   a. not perfect to look at. ☐
   b. perfectly created. ☐
2. When the Creator granted the horse its wish, the horse was
   a. extremely happy and grateful. ☐
   b. very sad and complained to the Creator. ☐
3. According to the horse, people would
   a. not appreciate his qualities, if he was a camel. ☐
   b. love him as a camel. ☐
4. The Creator wants us to be
   a. dissatisfied with our qualities and lives. ☐
   b. content with our lives and humble about our qualities. ☐
5. We must remember that
   a. all things on this earth are important and useful. ☐
   b. only some things on this earth are important and useful. ☐

B. Elucidate the quote, 'There is no respect for others without humility in one's self.' by Henri Frederic Amiel.

Relate

Tick the best options for these situations.

1. Your best friend is going to Spain for a holiday. You are going to visit your grandparents in another city. What would you do?
   a. throw a tantrum and complain to your parents' about it ☐
   b. explore your grandparents' city and have an exciting holiday ☐

2. It is your house help's son's first birthday and she invites you to a party at her home. What will you do?
   a. humbly thank her and give him a thoughtful birthday gift ☐
   b. not go the party as its not important ☐

3. You have bagged the first prize in a quiz contest. A participant from the contest asks you for some tips on how to be a good quizzer. What will you do?
   a. ignore the participant ☐
   b. politely give the participant a few useful tips ☐

4. Your uncle, visiting from Singapore, gifts you an expensive gaming console. You invite all your friends for an evening at your home. What will you do?
   a. enjoy and play with your friends ☐
   b. show-off and not let them touch it ☐

Act

Acting Game

We have the choice of being humble or arrogant in every situation. Follow the instructions to play this acting game.

1. Write the names of well-known superstars from films or sports on pieces of paper.
2. Fold the pieces of paper and put them in a bowl.
3. Form pairs. Each pair should pick up one piece of paper.
4. The pair has to act like the superstar whose name they pick. Pretend the superstar is being requested by a crowd of fans for autographs.

5. One partner must act as a proud superstar while the other must act like a humble superstar. You can use a humorous script to amuse your audience.

Happiness Box

Make Miss or Mr Courteous

- On a large piece of paper, draw a stick figure. Label the figure Mr or Miss Courteous.
- Write 'May I Help You?' on the shirt of your figure.
- Write courteous phrases such as 'Please tell me your troubles' or 'Sorry!' or 'Helping you is my pleasure, around the figure.
- Put this figure up in your room so that you are reminded every day about what you must do or say to be polite, courteous and friendly.

2. **Write a Diary Entry**

   Make a diary entry of incidents when you have been humble in the class or at home.

3. **Role-play**

   Form groups of 4 to 6 students. Enact in the class any one incident from the life of an eminent personality of India showcasing humble behaviour.

Teaching tips

- You may tell students how vanity always leads to a fall, while humility is a winner. Humble people are loved by everyone because they are not threatening.
- Tell students the story of Abraham Lincoln who never forgot his humble roots. You may also refer to Dr A. P. J. Abdul Kalam's life story.

3. Climate Change

Discuss

Read this news report and discuss in class the reasons behind this incident.

DAILY NEWS

No. 49,725 | THE BEST SELLING NEWSPAPER | Today's Edition

National - World - Business - Lifestyle - Travel - Technology - Sport - Weather

Three injured in leopard attack amid panic in Meerut

Meerut, 22 April: A team of forest officials is trying to tranquilize the wild cat which was last spotted in the JCO mess of Army in the Cantonment.

Three labourers working in an under-construction building in Fazalpur area in Cantonment were injured in an attack by a leopard, which has created panic in the city prompting authorities to shut down all schools on Wednesday.

Read along

Human beings have altered their environment in unprecedented ways. The sustainable development goal 13, Climate Action, raises awareness about human and institutional capacity on climate change mitigation. People must be empowered to become active citizens and use their power as consumers to demand more sustainable choices, and pressure governments and industry to take responsibility for their share of climate change.

13 CLIMATE ACTION

The seagull circled
    Above the darkened sea,
Helplessly watching
    Its child struggling to free
Its wing from the oil slick
    Now spread in the once azure sea.

The ship's crew watched
    Listlessly the fledgling's efforts to flee.
It was the bird's fault after all
    To swoop down to feed on dead fish
While they were trying
    To reduce fuel load.

It's an unwritten code
    That sea belonged to ships
And meant for human activities only.
    Man has the right to dump
All unwanted debris on blue water.
    Man should prosper.
Seabirds, penguins can no longer
    Thrive on resources from nature.

The mother seagull helplessly cried
    Seeing her child losing its fight for life.
The lifeless hungry young body
    Slowly sunk out of sight.
The crew laughed at the mother's plight.
    Loss of avian life wasn't blight
Man only should rule over the circle of life.

—Paromita Mukherjee Ojha

Think and Say

The vacant lot near your house is being cleared to build a mall. Sometimes, the gardener encounters snakes and small wild animals in your garden. He says, they have come from the vacant lot and must be killed. What will you do?

Remember

- Try to buy as many recyclable things you can.
- Plant trees and encourage others to do the same.
- Recycle paper waste generated in your house.
- Do not throw away things just because you don't need them. You can donate them.
- Urge you local government organizations to follow good waste management strategies.

Figure out

A. Tick the correct answers.

1. The seagull is circling above the ocean to
   a. look for fish to catch. ☐
   b. watch its baby struggle to escape the oil on the ocean surface. ☐
2. The oil slick has been created by
   a. the oil dumped by the ship's crew into the ocean. ☐
   b. oil rising from the ocean bed. ☐
3. The ship's crew is careless about poisoning the ocean because
   a. there are no living creatures in it. ☐
   b. they believe only human beings have the right to use all natural resources. ☐
4. The men laugh at the mother seagull's grief because
   a. they had never seen a seagull cry. ☐
   b. they believe other than human life no other lives are important on earth. ☐
5. The careless attitude of human beings will eventually
   a. destroy humanity as environmental balance is essential to sustain all life on Earth. ☐
   b. make them the rulers of the world. ☐

B. Write a poem on nature's beauty.

Relate

Tick the best options for these situations.

1. You see a fruit vendor packing fruits in polybags for his customers. What will you do?
   a. quietly take your fruits in a cloth bag and leave ☐
   b. explain to the vendor the harm polybags cause to the environment ☐

2. You have vounteered to check vehicles without pollution-free stickers in your city. Some drivers refuse to cooperate. What will you do?
   a. politely explain to the drivers the harm they are causing to the environment ☐
   b. avoid stopping aggressive drivers without the stickers ☐

3. You go to your village on a holiday and see people bathing, washing clothes, cleaning utensils and filling drinking water at the same river. What will you do?
   a. watch quietly because you are here for a short time ☐
   b. explain how they are polluting the river ☐

4. Your school encourages each class to maintain a part of the garden. So, once a week students of each class work on the small patch that is their responsibility. What will you do?
   a. take an active part in making the school ground green ☐
   b. make excuses so that you don't have to work ☐

Act

The Greenhouse Effect

Lets understand the Greenhouse Effect with the help of an experiment.

Materials required

- 2 thermometers
- 1 clear jar
- 1 stopwatch
- Sunlamp
- Observation sheet

Instructions

1. Work in groups.
2. Place the thermometers under the sunlamp until they are warm.
3. Record findings under Observation 1 on your observation sheets.
4. Place the jar over one of the thermometers for one minute and record findings under Observation 2.
5. Continue watching both thermometers and recording findings every minute for 10 minutes.

   Once the experiment is complete, all the students will talk about their findings.

Discuss how the air over the exposed thermometer changes temperature but the temperature of the air in the jar takes time to change

The light of the lamp is like the sunlight that warms the Earth's atmosphere. Without it the temperature would average a freezing zero degree.

Observe the air inside the jar. When gases such as carbon dioxide are released into Earth's atmosphere, they trap and absorb heat. This is called the Greenhouse Effect, a phenomenon which causes global warming and climate change.

Happiness Box

1. **To show your love for our Earth, here some things you can do.**
   - Use a recyclable water bottle and lunch bag at school.
   - Plant a tree in the school yard.
   - Recycle the paper you use at school.
   - Make a field trip to a local recycling centre.
   - Have an exhibition-cum-sale of recycled articles and give all proceeds go to an organization for endangered species.

2. **Cut out pictures that depict prevention of global warming from newspapers or magazines. Make a collage on a sheet of handmade paper and share it in class.**

3. **Match the following words with their descriptions.**

	Words	Descriptions
1.	Fauna	Process by which wastes are converted into new products and materials
2.	Ozone	The earth's resources that are used by living things for such needs as food, shelter, and manufacturing
3.	Recycling	The toxic air-polluting gas that causes acid rain
4.	Natural resources	The term used for increasing concentration of pesticides and other pollutants in the food chain
5.	Sulphur dioxide	The layer of the atmosphere that thins because of air pollution
6.	Biomagnification	A collective term for animals in the environment

Teaching tips

- Sensitize students to prudent usage of paper, wood, electricity and fuels to avoid wastage.
- Explain the concept of reducing carbon footfall.
- Mention that antiperspirants and deodorants contain aerosol which mixes with air and causes the thinning of the ozone layer.

4. Gulliver's Adventures

Discuss

Read about Anna Hazare's successful non-violent protest. Discuss the reasons for its success in class.

In 2011, Anna Hazare participated in the non-violent *satyagraha* movement for passing a stronger anti-corruption Jan Lokpal Bill in the Indian parliament. When the Prime Minister of India refused his demands, Hazare went on a peaceful fast.

Anna Hazare's non-violent protest attracted students, corporate executives, street vendors, pensioners, activists and even media to join the movement. The protest spread to all parts of the country. Within five days, the Government gave in to Hazare's demands.

Read along

Gulliver's Travels is a novel written by a famous author, Jonathan Swift. In his book, the author has mocked the customs of the English society of his times. Through Gulliver's adventures, Swift has also shown how life experiences can influence human nature.

Lemuel Gulliver is a married surgeon from Nottinghamshire, England, who has a penchant for travelling. He heads out on a fateful voyage to the South Seas, when he gets caught in a storm and is washed up on an island. This island, Lilliput, has a population of tiny people about six inches tall. They capture Gulliver as he sleeps and carry him to their capital city, where they keep him chained inside a large abandoned temple outside the city walls.

Gulliver becomes a great friend of the Emperor of Lilliput, who introduces Gulliver to many of their customs. For example, instead of staffing his cabinet with capable administrators, the Emperor chooses guys who perform best at a dangerous form of rope dancing. The Emperor asks Gulliver to help him in his war against Blefuscu, a similarly tiny kingdom across a channel of water. Gulliver agrees and because of his huge size, captures all of Blefuscu's navy.

These two men conspire to influence the Emperor to have Gulliver executed. They serve Gulliver with a series of Articles of Impeachment, with the final sentence that Gulliver is going to be blinded. Gulliver is informed of this plot against him by a friend at the Lilliputian court. He manages to escape to the island of Blefuscu. Fortunately for him, a human-sized boat washes ashore on Blefuscu. Gulliver rows to nearby Australia and finds a boat there to take him back to England.

Think and Say

You have some issues with your partner in class. Would you fight it out or bring it to the notice of the teacher and sort it out amicably?

Gulliver heads out to sea again after a brief stay in England with his family. Once again, a storm blows up, and Gulliver winds up on the island of Brobdingnag. The Brobdingnagians are sixty-foot tall giants, who treat Gulliver like an attraction at a fair. Gulliver comes to the attention of the Brobdingnagian Queen, who keeps him like a kind of pet. She is amused, because he is so tiny and yet manages to speak and act like a real person. This Queen employs a young girl, Glumdalclitch, to look after Gulliver and teach him their language. Glumdalclitch does this with great affection.

While Gulliver lives at the palace, he is constantly in danger—bees the size of pigeons nearly stab him, a puppy almost tramples him to death, a monkey mistakes him for a baby monkey and tries to stuff him full of food. As a result, Gulliver feels ridiculous all the time. He starts to lose his pride and self-importance acquired in Lilliput.

The Brobdingnagian King reinforces his new sense of humility. After Gulliver describes to him all that he can think of about English culture and history, the King of Brobdingnag decides that the English sound like tiny little pests. He absolutely refuses to accept Gulliver's gift of gunpowder because such weapons seem like an invitation to horrible violence and abuse.

When Gulliver thinks about the King's reaction, he realizes the foolishness of his own countrymen who indulge in such dangerous pursuits. It gives him a new perspective. Gulliver is humbled by the observation that the leader of a small island like Brobdingnag has realized that manufacturing weapons would only serve to trigger aggression. Violence or showing that one is violent invites more violence. It was such a simple fact but a great nation like England had been unable to perceive this. This was the reason that England had so many enemies.

Remember

- Being non-violent doesn't make one coward or weak.
- It takes courage to be non-violent in the face of violence.
- Non-violent action ensures your voice is heard.
- The outcome of non-violent is always constructive.

Figure out

A. Tick the correct answers.

1. What was Gulliver's response when the King of Lilliput requested him to help in the war against Blefuscu?
   a. Gulliver refused to help the King in such a violent activity. ☐
   b. Gulliver happily used his large size to help the King of Lilliput win the war. ☐
2. Were all the people at the court of Lilliput grateful to Gulliver for his help?
   a. The admiral and the treasurer hated Gulliver and plotted to blind him. ☐
   b. Each courtier of Lilliput showed their gratitude to Gulliver in words and action. ☐
3. When Gulliver was treated like a little wonder in Brobdingnag, how did he feel?
   a. Gulliver enjoyed being treated like a strange pet. ☐
   b. Gulliver was humbled when he realized his insignificance among the Brobdingnag. ☐
4. What did Gulliver learn from the King of Brobdingnag?
   a. Gulliver learnt that if one is violent, it invites aggression. ☐
   b. Gulliver learnt that one must use one's size to dominate. ☐
5. How did Gulliver realize that despite being a smaller nation than England, Brobdingnag was a wiser nation?
   a. Brobdingnag had more wise people than England. ☐
   b. Brobdingnag did not want weapons as it would invite violence. ☐

B. Write about an incident where something was achieved through non-violent means.

Relate

Tick the best options for these situations.

1. You have been given a penalty at your school football match, even though you did not break a rule. What would you do?
   a. shout and fight with the referee ☐
   b. explain patiently that it was not your fault ☐

2. Your younger sister and you had an argument. She makes an unnecessary complaint to your father. What would you do?
   a. react violently or with anger ☐
   b. tell your father your side of the story patiently ☐
3. Your best friend and you disagree and your friend says a lot of hurtful things to you. What will you do?
   a. confront her politely ☐
   b. turn violent and start a physical fight ☐
4. There is no water supply in your neighbourhood, a tanker is providing water. A fight breaks out in the crowd as everybody wants to fill their tanks first. What will you do?
   a. join in the fight because that is the only way you can get some water ☐
   b. stop people from fighting and request people to queue up ☐

Act

Non-Violent Movements

Mahatma Gandhi's movement for India's Independence and Martin Luther King Jr.'s movement for civil rights are two successful non-violent movements in history.

1. Form two teams—Mahatma Gandhi and Martin Luther King Jr.
2. Each team should answer the following questions and then discuss them.
   - Who were Mahatma Gandhi and Martin Luther King Jr.?
   - Why did they believe in non-violence?
   - Name the non-violent movements they led.
   - What changes did these movements bring about in the world?

Mahatma Gandhi

Martin Luther King Jr.

Happiness Box

1. **Let's make the peace symbol**

   Paint the peace symbol on the front and back of a white t-shirt.

   Wear the t-shirt and be a peace warrior.

   Find out other symbols associated with peace. You can also draw them on small cardboard sheets and make badges. Wear these badges or gift them to your friends.

2. **Tick 'P' for the pictures that symbolize peace and 'NP' for those that do not.**

P ☐ NP ☐

P ☐ NP ☐

P ☐ NP ☐

P ☐ NP ☐

P ☐ NP ☐

P ☐ NP ☐

P ☐ NP ☐

P ☐ NP ☐

Teaching tips

- Tell the students Gandhi's principle of non-violence giving example of the Dandi March.
- You may tell the story of Rosa Parks and the non-violent Montgomery civil rights protests.
- You may explain the meaning of the saying, 'When you are slapped on one cheek, offer your other cheek.'

5. The Bell of Justice

Discuss

Read the chart given below and discuss in class.

	Student Rights	Student Responsibilities
1.	I have the right to be treated with respect in school.	I must treat everyone in school with respect.
2.	I have the right not to be teased, hurt or made fun of in school.	I must not tease, hurt or make fun of anyone in school.
3.	I have the right to expect that the things I own will be safe at school.	I have the responsibility of not damaging the property of others or the school property.
4.	I have the right to work and play safely.	I have the responsibility to abide by the school rules and to play safely in supervised areas.
5.	I have the right to be told the truth.	I have the responsibility to be honest and truthful.
6.	I have the right to a clean, tidy, safe and comfortable school.	I have the responsibility to keep my school neat, clean, tidy and safe and to report any possible dangers.

Read along

The great Mughal Emperor Jahangir believed that true justice should always prevail in his kingdom. So he ordered a huge bell with a golden chain to be hung outside the *Diwan-i-Am* or Hall of Audience at the Agra Fort. It was called the 'Bell of Justice'. Anybody who wanted justice could ring the bell. The Emperor would give the person a hearing and ensure that justice was done.

One day, people saw a woman frantically ringing the bell. She was wailing, and two small children clung to her skirt. Emperor Jahangir ordered that she be brought into the Hall and asked her what the matter was.

With tears in her eyes, she said, 'Your Majesty, we are very poor. My husband cuts wood from the forest and sells it to give us one meal a day. This morning, when he went to the forest, an arrow struck him and he died. How will my children and I survive without him, *Jahanpanah*? What will we eat? Give us justice, Your Majesty'.

Jahangir said, 'Certainly, you will have justice. Do you know whose arrow killed your husband? The person who shot the arrow will have to pay with his life for the death of your husband. The law is very clear. An eye for an eye; a life for a life.'

The woman only kept crying silently.

Jahangir gently prodded her, 'Do not be afraid. Tell me, who killed your husband?'

The woman raised her tearful eyes to the King, and said, 'The arrow was shot by Empress Nur Jahan, *Jahanpanah*'.

The people gathered in the hall gasped.

Jahangir went pale. Then, he gathered himself and commanded, 'Call the Empress'. He turned to the frightened woman, 'If your story is true, you have the right to kill me in return. The law allows you that'.

'Nooo', came an anguished cry. Empress Nur Jahan rushed in and threw herself at the Emperor's feet. 'It was my arrow. I shall pay for it with my life not you'.

A loud murmuring ran through the listening crowd. Then the people parted, making way for an old man who walked through them. Everyone whispered, 'The *Qazi*! the *Qazi*!'

The old man was the Chief *Qazi* of the Kingdom. He said, '*Jahanpanah*, you have forgotten that the law also allows for blood money to be paid instead of a life. If the complainant agrees, then your weight in gold coins and jewels can be paid as compensation to her'.

The woman hurriedly said, 'Yes! Yes! I agree'.

The Emperor gently lifted Nur Jahan, who was still weeping. He said softly, 'Since the fault was yours, this blood money will be paid from your personal treasury and not the imperial *khazana*.'

The people in the Hall heaved a collective sigh of relief. Loud cheers filled the air praising Emperor Jahangir's just decision.

Think and Say

You find your classmate eating bananas and throwing the peels all over the school playground. When you object, she says, 'I have the right to eat in the school playground'. What will you do?

Remember

- Every human being deserves rights, no matter who they are or where they live.
- Everyone should have the right to safety, education, shelter, food, clothing, personal space and freedom of speech.
- Responsibility refers to the things we ought to do for others.
- Some of our responsibilities are following rules, standing up for others, caring for ourselves as well as others, and respecting the rights of others.

Figure out

A. Tick the correct answers.

1. The bell hung in Agra Fort was rung by people when
   a. they wanted to hear music. ☐ b. they wanted justice. ☐
2. When the woman's husband was killed by an arrow, she wanted
   a. justice from the Emperor. ☐ b. a job from the Emperor. ☐

3. The Emperor was determined to punish the wrongdoer because
   a. it was his responsibility to do so.
   b. he hated people hunting in the forest.
4. When the Emperor heard that the killer was Empress Nur Jahan, he
   a. forgave the wrongdoer because he loved her.
   b. offered his own life as he believed it was his duty to uphold the law.
5. When the woman agreed to take blood money, the Emperor
   a. was relieved that Empress Nur Jahan would not be punished.
   b. punished the Empress by making her pay the blood money from her own *khazana*.

B. Elucidate the words of Gary Haugen, 'Justice is doing for others what we would want done for us'.

Relate

Tick the best option for these situations.

1. You ride your new bicycle during the day. At the end of the day, the shining bicycle is muddy and dirty. What will you do?
   a. demand that a family member or a helper cleans it
   b. take time out to clean it
2. You invite your friends to watch cricket on TV. Your father makes snacks for all of you. What will you do after your friends leave?
   a. go to your room expecting your family members to clean up the room
   b. tidy the room and help your family by washing the dirty plates
3. You ate peanuts in a park. What will you do afterwards?
   a. collect the peanut shells in a bag to dispose of in a dustbin
   b. throw them on the grass
4. You are browsing books in the library and remove many of them to search for the books you want. What will you do after you find the books you need?
   a. arrange the books removed as they were on the shelf
   b. leave the books on library table and leave

Act

Living in a Community

1. Form teams of five students each.
2. Each team draws children playing in neighbourhood park or inside the building complex on a chart paper.
3. On the left-hand side of the drawing paper, write five rights of children in a neighbourhood.
4. On the right-hand side, write five responsibilities that the children must abide by.
5. After everyone finishes, put the charts up in the class.
6. Check how many of the rights have matching responsibilities. This shows that rights and responsibilities go hand in hand.

Happiness Box

1. **Tree of Rights and Responsibilities**

   On a green or a white chart paper, make a tree with branches and leaves.

   Cut out a leaf from the chart paper and write your name on it. On a note write a right and its corresponding responsibility.

   Stick the note to the leaf. Then, pin the leaf to one of the branches of the tree.

Teaching tips

- Stress that rights and responsibilities go hand in hand.
- You can enjoy rights only if you take the responsibility to ensure that everyone receives the benefits of those rights.
- Talk about the fundamental rights every Indian citizen has along with the duties enshrined in our Constitution.

6. Nelson Mandela

Discuss

Look at the pictures and discuss in class.

Was the fireman not afraid to enter a burning house?

Read along

Nelson Mandela was born in Transkei, South Africa on 18 July 1918. He was the son of a local tribal leader of the Tembu tribe.

However, unlike his father, Nelson Mandela studied at the University College of Fort Hare and the University of Witwatersrand.

Nelson was a good student and qualified with a law degree in 1942. He believed, 'Education is the most powerful weapon which you can use to change the world'.

During his time at University, he became increasingly aware of the racial inequality and injustice faced by black people in South Africa. This policy of segregation or discrimination based on race was called apartheid. In 1943, he decided to actively take part in the struggle to end apartheid.

In 1956, Nelson Mandela was arrested and charged with working against the government. After his prison sentence ended in 1961, Nelson Mandela suggested a guerilla resistance to apartheid.

In 1963, Mandela was again arrested and put on trial. This time, the State succeeded in convicting Mandela of plotting to overthrow the government. However, his case received a lot of international attention, and the apartheid regime of South Africa came under the glare of the world and international organizations. At the end of his trial, Nelson Mandela made a long speech, in which he spoke firmly of his belief in the principles of democracy.

Eventually, Nelson Mandela was released on 11 February 1990. The day was important for South Africa and the world. His release meant the end of apartheid. In April 1994, South Africa had its first full and fair elections, and Nelson Mandela became the first President of the new South Africa.

Nelson Mandela is the author of *Long Walk to Freedom,* his autobiographical work written and published in 1995. The book profiles his early life, coming of age, education and 27 years in prison.

Nelson Mandela was often referred to as Madiba—his clan name. Mandela said, 'I learned that courage was not the absence of fear, but the triumph over it. The brave man is not he who does not feel afraid, but he who conquers that fear.'

Think and Say

You are afraid of the dark. One rainy evening, you are alone at home and the electricity is switched off. What will you do?

Nelson Mandela retired from the presidency in 1999. He died on 5 December 2013 after a long illness, with his family at his side. He was 95 years old. The world is indebted to Mandela, as his struggle brought focus on discrimination based on race, colour, community and religion.

Remember

- Do the right thing, even if others oppose you.
- Deal with your daily challenges bravely.
- Be willing to try new things, even if you might fail.
- Tell the truth regardless of the consequences.
- Face your fears and learn to overcome them.
- Admit your mistakes and learn from them.
- Do not give in to negative pressure from friends.

Figure out

A. Tick the correct answers.

1. What was Nelson Mandela's belief about education?

   a. Mandela believed education was a waste of time. ☐

   b. Mandela believed that education can be used to change the world. ☐

2. Mandela knew he could be arrested, but was he afraid to oppose apartheid?

   a. He was afraid but he overcame his fear ☐

   b. He was fearless as he knew nobody could harm him. ☐

3. What was apartheid?

   a. segregation or discrimination based on race ☐

   b. segregation or discrimination based on education ☐

4. What is courage according to Mandela?

   a. Courage is conquering fear ☐

   b. Courage is the absence of fear ☐

5. Why is the world indebted to Nelson Mandela?

    a. He was the first President of South Africa. ☐

    b. His struggle highlighted discrimination based on colour, race, community and religion. ☐

B. 'The brave man is not he who does not feel afraid, but he who conquers that fear'. Find a real life story that exemplifies this statement.

Relate

Tick the best option for these situations.

1. You and your elder brother are playing in the park. Your brother argues with a group of older boys and you are afraid. What will you do?

    a. run off home because they might harm you ☐

    b. shout for help ☐

2. You are very shy and feel embarrassed to speak in front of your classmates. You are afraid that they may laugh if your reply is incorrect. What will you do?

    a. stay silent even though you know all the answers ☐

    b. swallow your fear and answer even if you may be laughed at ☐

3. During the school recess, you witness a senior student stealing from the science lab. You are afraid to report. What will you do?

    a. give in to your fear and keep quiet about the incident ☐

    b. report the wrongdoing ☐

4. At home, you fiddled with the TV, and now it is not working. Your father asks you and your brother if anybody had mishandled the device. What will you do?

    a. not own up to your carelessness ☐

    b. admit you had been careless ☐

Act

The Egg Charade

Materials required

- A wide-mouthed glass or jar
- Uncooked rice
- Egg

Method

For two teams with team leaders. The teams will perform charades in turns.

1. The team leader of Team A places the egg in the glass completely covered by rice. He or she explains that the egg represents someone hanging with a crowd of students.

2. The team leader will then give instructions and the team will have to silently act out the instructions without saying anything.

3. **Team leader:** My team is the group and the egg is a member of it. One day, the group starts making fun of other people. The egg doesn't like it so it tells them to stop. The leader taps the top of the glass rim. The egg rises up from the rice with each tap.

4. **Team leader:** The group starts excluding others from their games. The team leader taps the glass rim. The egg rises.

5. **Team leader:** They start telling lies. The team leader taps the rim. The egg rises.

6. **Team leader:** Each time, the egg refuses to go along with his friends and stands up for what's right, it rises higher. The team leader taps again.

7. When the egg has completely risen above the rice, the team leader and the team stop the charade.

   Team leader: It takes courage to do the right thing when others are not. A courageous person will rise to the top and stand out from the rest!

8. Now, the second team and its leader perform the Egg Charade. The Egg Charade proves the following truth.

A courageous person will rise to the top and stand out from the rest!

Happiness Box

1. **A Picture of Courage**

Draw a picture symbolizing courage. Give the picture a title by completing the sentence,

Courage is ....

....

Share your pictures in the classroom. You will enjoy discussing each classmate's idea.

2. **Write B for the actions that show bravery and C for those that show cowardice.**

	Action 1		Action 2	
1.	Classmates fighting	☐	Walking away from a fight	☐
2.	Teasing and bullying someone	☐	Standing up for someone who is being mistreated	☐
3.	Blaming others for your mistakes	☐	Accepting responsibility for your mistakes	☐
4.	Looking out only for yourself	☐	Helping others	☐
5.	Following the crowd	☐	Doing what's right even if alone	☐
6.	Quitting when things get tough	☐	Working hard, even when it's difficult	☐

Teaching tips

- Explain that it is all right to be afraid. All of us are afraid of something.
- Ensure that the students understand the difference between brave action and a foolhardy action.
- Explain that peer pressure can force one to take risks.

Happiness Activity

Clean environment and green spaces make us happy. They are good for our health and well-being too.

Let's take a look at what each of us can do reduce pollution.

Do's

1. Bin all waste if you are at an outing, near a water body.
2. Bury garden rubbish rather than burn it.
3. Carry a jute bag to the market.
4. Walk rather than drive to close-by places.
5. Segregate waste at source. That way, much of it can be recycled.
6. Grow a garden or keep potted plants to purify the air.
7. Try to carpool or use public transport.

Now write three things that keep the environment clean and at the same time make you happy.

....

....

....

....

....

....

....

....

....

Colour the poster. Circle the situations where air, water or the earth is being polluted.

BOOM
BOOMM
BOOM

In the word puzzle given below, circle 16 words related to the earth, its conservation and harmful effects of careless human actions.

S	R	O	P	O	L	L	U	T	I	O	N	L	M	H	J	U
R	Y	G	H	Y	U	G	X	C	H	E	M	I	C	A	L	S
A	Z	R	E	C	Y	C	L	I	N	G	S	G	R	J	U	Y
D	M	L	N	O	P	S	O	I	T	R	Q	A	B	S	L	P
I	B	G	V	H	G	U	D	W	B	V	X	V	B	L	N	H
A	J	I	I	O	P	L	M	K	A	C	I	D	R	A	I	N
T	O	M	R	L	G	D	P	Q	C	W	A	I	S	G	X	C
I	E	C	O	L	O	G	Y	U	T	I	O	S	P	G	F	D
O	M	A	N	A	X	E	D	X	E	F	U	P	I	O	M	J
N	I	R	M	V	J	U	N	K	R	A	Q	O	Z	O	N	E
U	S	B	E	I	O	L	O	V	I	E	J	S	K	P	U	N
R	S	O	N	A	L	E	E	T	A	I	L	A	O	P	T	Y
D	I	N	T	V	O	Y	M	G	R	K	E	L	A	H	S	H
N	O	M	P	E	S	T	I	C	I	D	E	O	P	J	U	B
H	N	B	S	E	E	N	A	A	S	U	K	H	I	P	L	O

Project I : Soda Bottle Greenhouse

Make a Garden in Your Home

You can grow plants in a bottle and watch leaves sprouting, roots growing out of seeds and flowers blooming.

Materials required

- 1 empty, washed and dry 2-litre soda bottle
- Sharp scissors
- Soil mixed with fertilizer
- Fruit or herb seeds that grow easily
- A plate to keep the greenhouse on

Steps

1. Carefully cut the soda bottle in half so that its lower part is deep enough to hold soil and plants.
2. Make a few holes in the lower part of the soda bottle for water to drain. Keep the upper part of the soda bottle and the lid.
3. Fill soil in the lower part of the soda bottle and sow the seeds. Water the soil lightly.
4. Put the upper part of the soda bottle back on the lower part. Tuck the edges of the upper part into the lower part. Make small slits in the upper part of the soda bottle to make it fit the lower part and leave the cap on.
5. Place your soda bottle garden on top of the plate in a sunny corner of the house and water regularly. The lid will retain moisture and heat and saplings will start to grow. As the walls of the soda bottle are transparent, you'll be able to watch the roots growing under the soil.
6. If your greenhouse has too much moisture, you will notice droplets of water on the walls. You can remove the lid for some time. When the plants get too big for the bottle, transplant them to your garden, and plant more seeds in the soda bottle.

Project II : The Lady with the Lamp

Gather information about Florence Nightingale, the Lady with the Lamp. Find out about her contribution to the field of nursing. Make a poster or a PowerPoint presentation on her work.

Your presentation should answer the following questions:

- Who was Florence Nightingale?
- What were the objectives of her work?
- What made her work unique for the times in which she lived?
- Why was she called, 'The Lady with the Lamp'?
- What have been Florence's contributions to the world?
- Find pictures of Florence Nightingale and a map showing the region she lived and worked in. Add some of Florence's thoughts expressed in her own words.

7. Icarus and Daedalus

Discuss

Read the poem and discuss the thoughts expressed by the poet in your class.

All Things Obey God

God's works are very great, but still
His hands do not appear:
Though heaven and earth obey His will,
His voice we cannot hear.

And yet we know that it is He
Who moves and governs all,
Who stills the raging of the sea,
And makes the showers fall.

Alike in mercy He bestows
The sunshine and the rain;
That which is best for us He knows,
And we must not complain.

Whether He makes His winds to blow,
And gives His tempests birth,
Or sends His frost, or bids the snow,
"Be thou upon the earth."

—Anonymous

Read along

Among all those mortals who grew so wise that they learned the secrets of the gods, none was more cunning than Daedalus.

He once built, for King Minos of Crete, a wonderful Labyrinth of winding ways. It was so cunningly tangled up and twisted around that, once inside, you could never find your way out again without a magic clue. But the king's favour veered with the wind, and one day, he had his master architect imprisoned in a tower. Daedalus managed to escape from his cell but it seemed impossible to leave the island, since every ship that came or went was well-guarded by order of the king.

Having watched the seagulls in the air, the only creatures that were sure of liberty, he thought of a plan for himself and his young son Icarus who was captive with him.

Little by little, he gathered a store of feathers great and small. He fastened these together with thread, moulded them in with wax, and fashioned two great wings like those of a bird. When they were done, Daedalus fitted them to his own shoulders, and after one or two efforts, he found that by waving his arms he could winnow the air and cleave it, as a swimmer does the sea. He held himself aloft, wavered this way and that with the wind, and at last, like a great fledgling, he learned to fly.

Without delay, he fell to work on a pair of wings for the boy Icarus and taught him carefully how to use them, bidding him to beware of rash adventures among the stars. 'Remember', said the father, 'never to fly very low or very high, for the fogs about the earth would weigh you down, but the blaze of the sun will surely melt your feathers apart if you go too near'.

Think and Say

Your parents tell you not to watch the latenight programme on TV as you have school the next day. What will you do?

For Icarus, these cautions went in through one ear and out by the other. Who could remember to be careful when he was to fly for the first time? Are birds careful? Not they aren't! And not an idea remained in the boy's head but the one of joy of escape.

The day came and the fair wind was to set them free.

The father put on his wings, and while the light urged them to be gone, he waited to see that all was well with Icarus, for the two could not fly hand in hand. Up they rose, the boy after his father. The hateful ground of Crete sank beneath them, and the country folk, who caught a glimpse of them when they were high above the treetops, took it for a vision of the gods, Apollo perhaps, with Cupid after him.

At first, there was a terror in the joy. The wide vacancy of the air dazed them, a glance downward made their brains reel. But when a great wind filled their wings, and Icarus felt himself sustained, like a halcyon-bird in the hollow of a wave, like a child uplifted by his mother, he forgot everything in the world but joy. He forgot Crete and the other islands that he had passed over. He saw though vaguely a winged thing in the distance before him that was his father Daedalus. He forgot his father's warnings. He longed for one draught of flight to quench the thirst of his captivity. He stretched out his arms to the sky and made towards the highest heavens.

Alas for him! Warmer and warmer grew the air. Those arms, that had seemed to uphold him, relaxed. His wings wavered, drooped. He fluttered his young hands vainly, he was falling, and in that terror, he remembered. The heat of the sun had melted the wax from his wings; the feathers were falling, one by one, like snowflakes; and there was none to help.

He fell like a leaf tossed down by the wind, down and down, with one cry that overtook Daedalus far away. When he returned, and sought high and low for the poor boy, he saw nothing but the bird-like feathers afloat on the water, and he knew that Icarus had drowned.

The nearest island, he named Icaria, in memory of the child; but he, in heavy grief, went to the temple of Apollo in Sicily, and there hung up his wings as an offering. Never again did he attempt to fly.

—Based on a Greek myth

Remember

- Obey your parents and respect their advice.
- Consider the reason for an instruction you dislike before you argue about it.
- Pay attention to what your teacher or your elders try to tell you. Think about it rationally and try to follow their advice.
- Never break rules concerning your or others' safety.
- Try to understand the reason for a rule.

Figure out

A. Tick the correct answers.

1. Daedalus tried to train his son to fly by
   a. letting him find out about the process by trial and error. ☐
   b. teaching him very carefully how to use the wings. ☐
2. The father told the son to remember that
   a. he could fly anywhere on the wings he had made. ☐
   b. he must not fly too low or too near the sun. ☐
3. Icarus treated his father's warnings as
   a. useless because he thought he could fly as carelessly as birds. ☐
   b. valuable as they would keep him safe while flying. ☐
4. When the wind filled Icarus' wings, he
   a. obeyed his father's instructions and kept following him. ☐
   b. forgot all the warnings and flew higher and closer to the sun. ☐
5. The result of Icarus' disobedience was that
   a. the feathers fell off his wings and Icarus drowned. ☐
   b. he came to be known as the only human who flew so close to the sun. ☐

B. Write the difference between 'real obedience' and 'blind obedience'.

Relate

Tick the best options for these situations.

1. All your friends perform tricks with their cycles on the road like riding without holding the handle bars. Your parents have strictly instructed you to never do it. What will you do?
   a. act like your friends when you are away from home ☐
   b. obey your parents ☐

2. You have to walk a short distance to your school and on the way you pass an intersection with traffic lights. You hate waiting for the lights to change. What will you do?
   a. break the traffic rules and run across the road while the traffic is moving ☐
   b. wait for the light to change and the traffic to stop before crossing the road ☐

3. During recess, as a school prefect, you go around the school, ensuring everyone throws waste in the bin. Later, you are alone in the corridors and unwrapping a bar of chocolate. What will you do?
   a. through the wrapper in the bin no matter what ☐
   b. carelessly throw the wrapper on the floor ☐

4. You are part of a school group visiting a wild life sanctuary. Your teacher gives strict instructions that after dark, nobody must go outside the sanctuary guest house as wild animals may be around. What will you do?
   a. disobey your teacher and decide to go exploring with your friends ☐
   b. obey your teacher and convince your friends to do the same ☐

Act

Game of Obedience

1. Work in pairs
2. Each pair must stand with one student facing the wall.
3. The other student stands one foot behind the first student facing his or her back.

4. The first student must keep eyes closed.
5. When the second student says, 'fall', the first student should free fall backwards.
6. The second student must instantly hold his or her partner and not let the student crash to the floor.
7. Now, the pair can change their roles.

Happiness Box

Bunch of Obedience Keys

Materials required

- Stiff white paper
- Scissors
- Hole puncher
- Black marker
- Red twine or wire

Method

1. Cut the paper in the shape of keys.
2. On the curved upper part of all the keys, write the word O-B-E-Y.
3. On the lower part of each of the four keys, write one of the following ways to obey:
   - Instantly
   - Cheerfully
   - Completely
   - Without complaining
4. Now, punch holes in the centre of the upper part of the keys and thread the twine or wire through them. Twist and tie it. You have a bunch of obedience keys.

3. **Design a poster called 'Be Safe on the Road'. Write at least six rules that we must obey on the road. Decorate the poster and share it in class.**

Teaching tips

- Explain that obedience is applicable to everyone, not just children or students. Give examples of how adult disobedience can create chaos in society.
- Explain that not all the people in authority can be obeyed completely. Only those who can be trusted should be obeyed.
- Young children need to be alert and careful at all times regarding what they are expected to obey.
- Also, explain that one must judge whether one is being asked to do the right or wrong thing. Blind obedience should be discouraged.

8. Eagle-Eyed Leon

Discuss

Look at the pictures and discuss in class.

Read along

THE SUN

SCHOOLBOY CATCHES THIEF WITH A CAN OF LEMONADE

MANCHESTER, JUNE 22

Eagle-eyed Leon Yates, 12, was on his way home from school last month when he spotted two men acting suspiciously outside a neighbour's home.

He saw them entering the unlocked property and stealing a woman's handbag while their victim was in the back garden. After alerting his mother and neighbour, Leon drove around with them, looking for the thief who had already fled the scene. When he returned home, he spotted an empty can of lemonade that the thief had been drinking from. Quick thinking Leon carefully bagged the can up for evidence without touching it.

DNA from the vital find, along with Leon's detailed description of the culprit, enabled police to arrest and charge prolific burglar and drug addict, Daniel Jones. Jones was jailed yesterday after pleading guilty to the offence.

Schoolboy Leon earned a reward of chocolates from his 59-year-old neighbour.

Leon of Breightmet in Bolton, Greater Manchester, hopes to become a policeman after leaving school. He said, 'I hope to catch a few more'.

Jones, 26, of Bolton, was jailed for two years and five months at Bolton Crown Court.

Speaking about Leon's actions, his neighbour, who did not wish to be named, said, 'He is really wonderful. I can't thank him enough.'

Deputy Chief Inspector Paul Hitchin, head of Bolton CID, called Leon's quick-thinking '...an absolutely superb bit of detective work'. He added, 'I will be putting Leon forward for a commendation from the police'.

Think and Say

You are walking on the road and a boy running on the road pushes an old lady carrying a shopping basket. The lady is fine but all the things from her basket are scattered on the road. What will you do?

Remember

- Ask family members what you can do to help them.
- Practise listening to people. Sometimes, people just need to be heard.
- Sometimes, people may be lonely. Show them you care by calling them.
- Volunteer to work at an old age home or coach street children.
- Donate money, clothes, medicines or toys.

Figure out

A. Tick the correct answers.

1. What did Leon do when he saw two men behaving suspiciously in front of his neighbour's house?
   a. He observed them closely. ☐
   b. He went on his way as it did not concern him. ☐
2. Why did Leon look for the thief first and then pick up the lemonade can?
   a. He spotted the lemonade can later. ☐
   b. He wanted to find his neighbour's stolen handbag first. ☐
3. Was Leon proud that he had been rewarded by his neighbour and will get a police commendation?
   a. He was satisfied that the thief was caught. ☐
   b. He boasted to his friends about his reward. ☐
4. Why does Leon want to be a police officer when he grows up?
   a. so that he can help people ☐
   b. because he wants a good job ☐
5. Why would Paul Hitchin recommend Leon for a police commendation?
   a. because he came to know that Leon wants to be a policeman ☐
   b. because he appreciated Leon's intelligence and desire to help people ☐

B. Often we are told, 'Just mind your own business. Don't get involved in any trouble on the street. That way you will be safe'. Do you think real life heroes would exist if all of us held this attitude?

Relate

Tick the best options for these situations.

1. You are travelling in a crowded bus but you have a seat. An old lady enters the bus. You look around and there is no vacant seat. What will you do?
   a. ignore her and look out of the window as you sat down first ☐
   b. instantly stand up and offer her your seat ☐
2. A new student has joined your class, a few months after the term had begun. He is finding it difficult to keep pace with the rest of the class. What will you do?
   a. offer him your notes for the lessons he has missed ☐
   b. not help him as its not your concern ☐
3. While walking to school, you see a student of another school falling off his bicycle. He is bruised and needs help. What will you do?
   a. walk away because you don't know him ☐
   b. help him up, pick up his cycle and see him safely off to school ☐
4. You are in the market buying fruits from a vendor, when two boys steal a couple of mangoes from the vendor's cart and run away. What will you do?
   a. shrug and complete your purchases ignoring the vendor's complaints ☐
   b. try to help the vendor by calling for help ☐

Act

We Help

Make a WE HELP group in your neighbourhood.

Go around your neighbourhood and observe if any of your neighbours need help. It could be an elderly person who might need help putting washed clothes on a clothes line or a mother with a small baby who might need some shopping to be done.

Your WE HELP group can help them with these chores.

Your actions will make your neighbours happy and make you feel contented.

Happiness Box

With My Own Two Hands

Materials required

- Thick chart paper
- Watercolour paints
- Markers

With my Own Two Hands

I can make the world
a better place
I can do kind deeds
I can help people
I can do the best I can.
With my own two hands

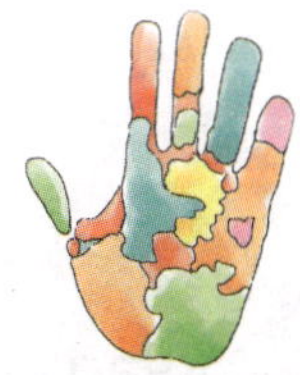

Method

1. Paint your palms with all the colours you like. Paint each finger a different colour and your palm with multiple colours.
2. On the chart paper make two hand prints, 12 inches apart.
3. On the top of the prints write: With My Two Hands
4. Under it write six things that you can do with your two hands. For example, make the neighbourhood a better place or help my friend
5. Draw a beautiful border all around your poster and share it in the class.

2. Say a short story about helping people. Write the incident that touched your heart the most.

Teaching tips

- Clarify that helping others is a selfless activity. If one acts because one expects something in return, it cannot be called helping.
- Explain that the help offered must be welcome. With the intent of helping, one cannot force oneself on somebody or invade their privacy.
- You may give contacts of organizations where students can volunteer to help people in need.

9. Where the Mind is Without Fear

Discuss

Read and discuss in class.

Do you believe freedom is the birthright of all living beings on earth?

Then, is it justified to keep birds and animals in cages, use mice and other animals for scientific experiments and poach animals for skin and medicines.

Read along

Where the mind is without fear and the head is held high
Where knowledge is free
Where the world has not been broken up into fragments
By narrow domestic walls
Where words come out from the depth of truth
Where tireless striving stretches its arms towards perfection
Where the clear stream of reason has not lost its way
Into the dreary desert sand of dead habit
Where the mind is led forward by thee
Into ever-widening thought and action
Into that heaven of freedom, my Father, let my country awake

—Rabindranath Tagore

Think and Say

Your parents have asked you to browse the Internet for your studies. They trust you not to use this freedom to access social media while studying.
What will you do?

Remember

- Freedom is the birthright of all living beings.
- We are really not free until our minds are free from fear.
- Only by being free of petty thoughts can we live a dignified life.
- When we receive the privilege of being truly free, we must return the gift by working hard to achieve perfection.
- We must be grateful for the gift of freedom because there are many in this world who don't have it.
- We must always respect freedom and never misuse it.

Figure out

A. Tick the correct answers.

1. We can respect ourselves when we
   a. do not fear anything. ☐ b. feel fear in our minds. ☐
2. We are free to move anywhere when
   a. different countries in the world give us permission. ☐
   b. the world is not divided by people who have petty thoughts. ☐
3. People progress only when
   a. they work hard to make themselves and their work perfect. ☐
   b. they work hard to earn more and more money. ☐
4. Both thoughts and actions are noble when
   a. people view everything with suspicion. ☐
   b. people view everything with reason and logic. ☐
5. People enjoy real freedom when they can live
   a. as other people want them to. ☐
   b. as they want to. ☐

B. The poem 'Where the Mind is Without Fear' encourages us to choose a path where we are not afraid of our actions and our head is held high. Write about an incident in which you acted wisely.

Relate

Tick the best option for these situations.

1. Your parents trust you and give you the freedom of studying at your friend's home for a test. What will you do?
   a. misuse the freedom to go off to the park to play
   b. respect the freedom and study at your friend's home
2. Your class teacher allows you the freedom of coming late to her class because you are practising for the interschool football match. What will you do?
   a. run to class as soon as your practice is over
   b. misuse the freedom by roaming in the corridors before going to class
3. You have the freedom of expressing your views in your family. What will you do?
   a. respect that freedom by politely expressing your views
   b. argue and voice loudly your disagreement with your family

Act

Form two debating teams in your class. Present arguments for and against the motion: 'Domesticating animals encroaches on the freedom of the animals'.

Happiness Box

1. **Research on the Internet and find the story of a teenager who participated in the freedom struggle of India. Gather information about the person and put it together in the form of a PowerPoint presentation and share it with the class.**
2. **Write a poem or a song about freedom.**

Teaching tips

- Explain that freedom means being free to choose, yet many a time it is best to take the advice of parents or teachers before making a choice because they have more experience.
- Remind students that suffering injustice silently is cowardice. One must always speak up against injustice.

10. Charlie Brown and Franz Stigler

Discuss

Look at the pictures and discuss in class.

Read along

It was 1943, and World War II was raging. The Americans had finally joined the war. An American pilot, Charles 'Charlie' Brown was stationed in England with a squadron of Flying Fortresses. On 20 December, his squadron had the task of bombing Bremen in Germany.

Brown's B-17 began its 10-minute bomb run at 27,300 ft. But before the bomber released its bomb load, accurate anti-aircraft fire had shattered its front, knocked out and damaged two engines. The engines had to be throttled back so that they did not speed up. This damage slowed down the bomber considerably. Brown could not remain with his formation and fell back. Soon his B-17 was the lone bomber and easily became the target for sustained enemy attacks.

For nearly ten minutes, a dozen enemy fighter planes attacked Brown's lagging B-17. Number three engine was also damaged and could only give out half power. The gunner's weapon jammed and the crew was badly wounded. Brown, himself had got hit in his right shoulder. The morphine capsules onboard had frozen, so nobody could use them for first-aid. The radio had been destroyed, and the bomber's exterior was badly damaged.

The crippled B-17 was spotted by the Germans on ground as well as by a German ace fighter pilot, Franz Stigler in his Messerschmitt Bf 109 G-6. He quickly came alongside Brown's plane. Through the damaged bomber's airframe, Stigler was able to see the injured and incapacitated crew. Brown was surprised when the German fighter plane did not open fire on them.

Observing the B-17, Stigler recalled the words of one of his commanding officers, Gustav Rödel, when fighting in North Africa, 'You are a fighter pilots first, last, always. If I ever hear of any of you shooting at someone in a parachute, I'll shoot you myself.'

Stigler later commented, 'To me, it was just like they were in a parachute. I saw them and I couldn't shoot them down.'

Two times, Stigler tried to signal to Brown to land at a German airfield and surrender or divert to nearby neutral Sweden, where he and his crew would receive medical treatment and be interned the remainder of the war. Brown did not understand Stigler's signals and flew on.

Stigler kept flying close to the damaged B-17 in a formation so that German anti-aircraft did not target it. He escorted the American plane over the coast until it reached the open seas. Once, he was certain that the bomber was out of German airspace, Stigler departed with a salute.

Brown managed to fly the 250 miles across the North Sea and land his plane at the airfield in England. At the after-flight meeting, he informed his officers about how a German pilot had let him go. They told him not to publicize it as Germans were the enemy in this war. Stigler said nothing of the incident to his commanding officers, knowing that a German pilot who spared the enemy while in combat risked execution.

After the war, Charlie Brown started an extensive search for Stigler. Finally, the two pilots met each other after 40 years. They developed a friendship and a strong bond that lasted till Franz Stigler's death in March 2008.

Think and Say

You see a man shouting at a street child for cleaning his car without permission at a traffic crossing. What will you do?

Remember

- Avoid having preconceived ideas and prejudices.
- Don't think what is different about people instead look for similarities.
- Try to put yourself into another person's shoes and imagine that person's life.
- Be a patient and alert listener.
- Open up to other people.
- Think of ways to help others.

Figure out

A. Tick the correct answers.

1. When Brown's plane was damaged and fell back, what did the enemy fighters do?
   a. They pitied the damaged plane and let it fly back to England.
   b. They attacked it mercilessly.
2. Why did Franz Stigler come alongside Brown's damaged plane?
   a. He wanted to see the people inside the plane before attacking it.
   b. He wanted to help Brown and his crew.
3. Why did Stigler not shoot at Brown's plane?
   a. Brown was Stigler's friend and he could not shoot his friend.
   b. Stigler could not shoot at helpless people even if they were his enemy.
4. Why do you think Stigler would have been executed?
   a. During war, it was your duty to kill the enemy and not be humane
   b. During war, it was a crime if you missed your mark of hitting your enemy.
5. Why did Charlie Brown search for Stigler after the war?
   a. Charlie wanted to kill Stigler as he was the enemy.
   b. Charlie could not forget Stigler's humanity that saved his and the crew's lives and wanted to thank him.

B. Why is humanity important during times of war? Write an argument to support your view.

Relate

Tick the best options for these situations given below.

1. On a cold winter evening, you see a small street child sitting outside your home shivering. What will you do?
   a. ignore the child as you cannot help all the street children
   b. give the child some warm food and clothes

2. Members of a charity organization are collecting old clothes to donate in a disaster-hit region. They come to your home and you open the door. What will you do?
   a. give them as many old clothes as you can find in your home and then join them ☐
   b. tell them you are too busy to waste your time and shut the door ☐
3. As you come to the playground during recess, a little child runs past and falls down. His knee starts bleeding. What will you do?
   a. give the child a glance and then walk away with your friends ☐
   b. ask your friends to help you take the injured child to sick room ☐
4. Some shelters for the poor near your school are gutted in a fire. Your class decides to collect money to donate to the homeless. You have only ten rupees which is to buy a snack during recess. What will you do?
   a. tell your teacher that you have no money to donate ☐
   b. donate your ten rupees and share your friend's lunch during recess ☐

Act

Someone Else's Shoes

1. Pick up any of these character cards
2. Pair up with a classmate, and read your card aloud while your partner practises being an empathic listener.
3. Switch roles, practise being empathic as your partner plays the character and tells you what he or she is experiencing.

Character Cards

Marcus is a star quarterback on the school football team. During one of the final games of the season, he was injured so badly that he couldn't play in the rest of the games, nor could he go to school for three months.

Chen always admired her friend Lily's wardrobe. One day, when they were hanging out at Lily's house, Chen asked to borrow Lily's expensive blue sweater. Lily said she could, but then made fun of Chen, telling everyone at school that Chen couldn't afford her own nice clothes.

Anita's best friend confided in her about a surprise birthday party she had planned to throw for her brother. Anita accidentally let the secret slip, and now her best friend won't talk to her.

Happiness Box

1. **'I Am Human' Badge**

Materials required

Coloured papers, cardboard, glue, compass, mountain tape, scissors, safety pins, stickers, ruler

Method

1. Start by cutting your first sheet of paper (15 cm × 8 cm) twice. Then cut your matching paper (10 cm × 2.5 cm) twice for the ribbons.
2. Draw a 4 cm diameter circle on the cardboard using the compass and cut it out.
3. Using the first cutting, accordion fold both paper strips with 1 cm spacing.
4. Fold each paper in half and stick them to form a semi circle.
5. Then stick both to make a full circle.
6. Turn over and stick a small piece of tape. Then stick the cardboard on it. Use the ribbon papers strips and stick on the piece of cardboard.
7. Insert the safety pin in a piece of paper and stick to the back.
8. Repeat on the other side, but instead of sticking the ribbon and safety pin, put a sticker that has a smiley or your favourite emoticon saying: I AM HUMANE

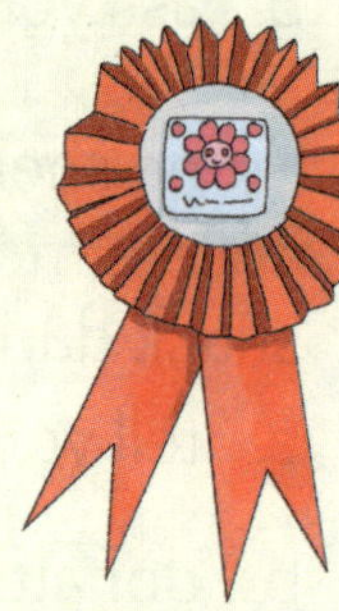

Are You Empathic?

2. **Circle 'Yes' if the sentence describes you, or 'No' if it does not.**

1.	I often think about other people's feelings.	Yes	No
2.	I don't make fun of other people because I can imagine what it feels like to be in their shoes.	Yes	No
3.	I listen to others about what they're going through.	Yes	No
4.	I try to understand other people's point of view.	Yes	No
5.	I am aware that not everyone reacts to situations the same way as I do.	Yes	No

Teaching tips

- Explain how it is important to observe people's body language that tells us how they feel.
- It is important to be empathetic towards people without pretensions, else one will end up offending them.

11. Mohun's Triumph

Discuss

Read the following anecdote and discuss in class.

Addressing a group of management students at a premier institute, the owner of a global corporate company asked, 'How many of you believe that your admission to this Institute was solely due to your own efforts?'

A few hands went up. He continued, 'All those hands that are up, don't bother to apply to my company. I will never let you set foot inside it'.

He explained his drastic statement, saying, 'Tell me that your parents did not help you get a good school education that was a base for your admission. Tell me that your teachers did not teach you all you needed to know. Tell me that your siblings did not help you in various ways to pass your exams. Above all, tell me that the people who examined your entrance test and interview here did not do their duty fairly and honestly.'

The students were overwhelmed.

'So if you start thinking of how many people really contributed to your presence in this Institute, you will find many, many more than those I have mentioned. Send up a prayer of thanks to them. Your work was only a part of a huge collaborative effort to get you here.'

Read along

News Times

106 YEARS AGO MOHUN BAGAN'S TRIUMPH CHANGED INDIAN HISTORY

SUTAPA DAS

July 29

Aamir Khan's movie *Lagaan* is a milestone in Indian cinema. It is a brilliant portrayal of the angst of the farmers against the oppressively dominating British empire. To be released from the obligation of paying taxes or *lagaan* that year, the farmers agreed to a cricket match against the British. But there were conditions; if the British team won the match, three times the tax would be imposed on the farmers while a victory for the Indians would mean an exemption from tax for three years. The conclusion of this film is that the farmers become winners of the match. So they free themselves from the tax and the British.

However, the events all of us saw on reel actually took place in real life too. A similar incident involved the Mohun Bagan Football Club, one of the oldest football clubs in Asia. It is an unbelievable story of how Mohun Bagan had their '*Lagaan* moment' on July 29, 1911.

It was the beginning of the 20th century, and the situation in Bengal was very tense. In 1905, Lord Curzon had partitioned Bengal, and there was tension everywhere. The demand for independence was again revived. This time, the British were firmly on the back foot. It was against this backdrop, that a match between Mohun Bagan and the British Army's East Yorkshire Regiment was arranged and its consequence changed the entire landscape of India.

Shibdas Bhaduri was the captain of Mohun Bagan team, which was set up in 1889. Its players played barefoot. The match against the East Yorkshire Regiment was played in front of about 80,000 fans. The East Yorkshire team scored first but Mohun Bagan's skipper fought back equalizing it. The entire Indian team was well-knit. Each team member was alert to capitalize on every opportunity presented to them. They were a perfect example of teamwork and collaborated effort. Finally, the watershed moment came when Abhilash Ghosh showed his potential on a pass from Bhaduri. Guarded by his team mates and with tremendous skill, he netted the winning goal.

Jubilantly, the crowd erupted. They were screaming with triumphant joy. Wild celebrations were held right on the field. Just on cue, it started raining. Gradually, the drenched team and spectators realized an unbelievable fact. Mohun Bagan had become the first Indian team to win the IFA Shield Trophy!

This win by Mohun Bagan changed the way India thought and acted in many ways. Since then, July 29 has been celebrated as Mohun Bagan team Day. It was from that day that the freedom movement was given a new lease of life and intensity.

This win fired the entire country with inspiration. The energy it released made the British media pen down the sentiment in one line: *'What the Congress failed to achieve, Mohun Bagan has'.*

It has been 106 years since that glorious day, but the achievements of Mohun Bagan continue to stand the test of time.

Think and Say

You along with four other classmates have been allocated a group project. How will you ensure that each student will do their share of work on time?

Remember

When people collaborate:

- work gets done faster.
- there is more creativity.
- a team is created for future projects.
- more solutions are available to problems.
- there is more learning.
- there are more methods or techniques to achieve a goal.
- there is more flexibility.
- risks are shared.
- it is more fun to work.

Figure out

A. Tick the correct answers.

1. How was the story of *Laagan* similar to the Mohun Bagan incident?
   a. Both were about exemption of taxes from the British in India ☐
   b. Both were about how a collaborated effort can lead to victory ☐

2. Why were the Mohun Bagan team barefoot?
   a. The team could not afford football shoes ☐
   b. The team played better without wearing shoes ☐

3. Although the Mohan Bagan team looked weak, what was their strength?

   a. Their hatred for the Yorkshire team

   b. Their team spirit that made them turn every opportunity into a win

4. How did Mohun Bagan football team winning the IFA trophy influence the rest of India?

   a. Every Indian started learning football

   b. Every Indian realized that no task is impossible with a collaborative effort

5. What did the British media mean by, 'What the Congress failed to achieve, Mohun Bagan has'.

   a. It meant that Mohun Bagan had joined the freedom struggle

   b. It meant that Mohun Bagan served to unite all the Indians in their struggle to achieve Independence from the British

B. Write an essay illustrating this thought.

'Unity is strength... when there is teamwork and collaboration, wonderful things can be achieved.'

—Mattie Stepanek

Relate

Tick the best options for these situations.

1. Your pet dog found the gate open and wandered out. You should search for him in the neighbourhood before he reaches the main road. What will you do?

   a. request all your friends to help you search your pet

   b. hesitate in taking help and search all by yourself

2. Your school has asked all the students to collect warm clothes for street children from their neighbourhoods. What will you do?

   a. do it alone even though you find it difficult to ask people to donate clothes

   b. request your neighbourhood friends to help you as it' s fun to do things together

3. There are plans to turn your colony park into a shopping area. Your friends and you want to protest. What will you do?

   a. go by yourself to the colony office to protest even though you know it won't carry much weight ☐

   b. go to the office with your family and friends to raise a collective voice to protest ☐

4. All your friends like to play table tennis, but you don't have the right sports equipment for it. What will you do?

   a. buy the equipment using the money contributed by your friends and you ☐

   b. pressurize your parents to buy the equipment for you and your friends ☐

5. You are the class monitor. Your teacher has instructed you to tidy up and decorate your classroom for the 'Clean Class' contest. What will you do?

   a. stay back late in school to the job by yourself and still not be able to finish it on time ☐

   b. divide the jobs amongst groups who will make the class so beautiful that you win the contest ☐

Act

Keep It Up

1. Divide the class in groups of ten students each. Let one student be the counter who does not join any group.
2. Each group stands in a circle holding hands.
3. A balloon is dropped in the centre of each group.
4. The goal is to see how many times does each group, while holding hands, push the balloon up in the air to keep it afloat.
5. The counter starts counting. If the balloon touches the ground, the group must start afresh.
6. Students may tap the balloon with hands, arms, heads, shoulders, chests, or knees but not feet.
7. The group that keeps the balloon afloat for the longest count is the winner.

Happiness Box

1. Make a floor mosaic with lentils and grains

Materials required

Cardboard, glue, brush, different types of lentils, black cumin seeds

Method

1. Take a thick cardboard of 12 x 12 inches and draw a pattern on it.
3. Apply glue over each part of the drawing using a brush.
4. Scatter lentils or grains very closely on the glued part as per the colour you want it to be.
5. Create the mosaic by filling all the parts with differently coloured lentils and grains.
6. Let the glue dry properly.
7. Once your floor mosaic is ready, place at in the centre of the floor as a decoration.

2. Write four reasons for why you like working in a group.

Teaching tips

- If there are disagreements in a team, they must be discussed politely. Anger and quarreling have no place in team work.
- Team spirit and standing up for one another is essential for the success. When things go wrong, the team together takes responsibility without pointing fingers at individual teammates.

12. Make a Difference

Discuss

Anu's mother is sick. She decides to help her mother. Look at the help wheel and discuss in class.

Anu's Help Wheel

Read along

At the word 'telegraph', Mrs March snatched it, read the two lines it contained, and dropped back into her chair as white as if the little paper had sent a bullet to her heart. Laurie dashed downstairs for water, while Meg and Hannah supported her, and Jo read aloud, in a frightened voice . . .

TELEGRAPH

Mrs. March

Your husband is very ill. Come at once.

S. HALE

Blank Hospital, Washington.

How still the room was as they listened breathlessly, how strangely the day darkened outside and how suddenly the whole world seemed to change, as the girls gathered about their mother, feeling as if all the happiness and support of their lives was about to be taken from them.

For several minutes, there was nothing but the sound of sobbing in the room, mingled with broken words of comfort, tender assurances of help, and hopeful whispers that died away in tears. Poor Hannah was the first to recover, 'The Lord keep the dear man! I won't waste no time a-cryin', but get your things ready right away, mum'.

'She's right, there's no time for tears now. Be calm, girls, and let me think.'

They tried to be calm, poor things, as their mother sat up, looking pale but steady, and put away her grief to think and plan for them.

The short afternoon wore away. All other errands were done, and Meg and her mother busy at some necessary needlework, while Beth and Amy got tea, and Hannah finished her ironing. But still Jo did not come. They began to get anxious. Laurie went off to find.

She came walking in with a very queer expression of countenance, for there was a mixture of fun and fear, satisfaction and regret in it. It puzzled

the family as much as did the roll of bills she laid before her mother, saying with a little choke in her voice, 'That's my contribution toward making Father comfortable and bringing him home!'

'My dear, where did you get it? Twenty-five dollars! Jo, I hope you haven't done anything rash?'

'No, it's mine honestly. I didn't beg, borrow, or steal it. I earned it, and I don't think you'll blame me, for I only sold what was my own.'

As she spoke, Jo took off her bonnet, and a general outcry arose, for all her abundant hair was cut short.

'Your hair! Your beautiful hair!'

'Oh, Jo, how could you? Your one beauty.'

'My dear girl, there was no need of this.'

'She doesn't look like my Jo any more, but I love her dearly for it!'

Jo assumed an indifferent air, which did not deceive anyone, and said, rumpling up the brown bush and trying to look as if she liked it, 'It will be good for my vanity, I was getting too proud of my wig. It will do my brains good to have that mop taken off. My head feels deliciously light and cool, and the barber said I could soon have a curly crop, which will be boyish, becoming, and easy to keep in order. I'm satisfied, so please take the money and let's have supper.'

'Tell me all about it, Jo. I am not quite satisfied, but I can't blame you, for I know how willingly you sacrificed your vanity, as you call it. But, my dear, it was not necessary, and I'm afraid you will regret it one of these days,' said Mrs March.

'No, I won't!' returned Jo stoutly, feeling much relieved that her prank was not entirely condemned.

'What made you do it?' asked Amy who just couldn't believe that Jo had willingly let go of her hair.

'Well, I was wild to do something for Father,' replied Jo, as they gathered about the table, for healthy young people can eat even in the midst of trouble. 'I hate to borrow as much as Mother does, and I knew Aunt March would croak, she always does, if you ask for a ninepence. Meg gave all her quarterly salary towards the rent, and I got nothing but few clothes. I felt miserable and wanted to do any possible thing to contribute.

'You needn't feel miserable, my child! You had no winter things and got the simplest with your own hard earnings,' said Mrs. March with a look that warmed Jo's heart.

'Didn't you feel dreadful when the first cut came?' asked Meg, with a shiver.

Think and Say

There is a strong dust storm at night and the next morning at school, teachers and students find dust piled on the floor. The principal asks students to volunteer to help. What will you do?

'I took a last look at my hair while the man got his things, and that was the end of it. I never snivel over trifles like that. I will confess, though, I felt queer when I saw the dear old hair laid out on the table, and felt only the short rough ends of my head. It almost seemed as if I'd an arm or leg off. The woman saw me look at it, and picked out a long lock for me to keep. I'll give it to you, Marmee, just to remember past glories by, for a crop is so comfortable I don't think I shall ever have a mane again'.

Mrs March folded the wavy chestnut lock and laid it away with a short gray one in her desk. She only said, 'Thank you, deary', but something in her face made the girls change the subject, and talk as cheerfully as they could about Mr Brooke's kindness, the prospect of a fine day tomorrow, and the happy times they would have when Father came home to be nursed.

—Adapted from Little Women by Louisa M Alcott

Feelings and Emotions

Communication

Our feelings and emotions determine our reactions to situations and people. While we cannot control our emotions, we can control how we feel. It is our gut feeling that tells us what is right and what is wrong for us. Emotions or feelings often get converted into actions, which can be safe or unsafe, healthy or unhealthy. Actions have consequences too. It is essential to know how to express our feelings or emotions, especially in uncomfortable situations. While expressing happy emotions is easy, expressing sadness, anger, disappointment, rejection, or embarrassment can be difficult to communicate. However, we should never hesitate from expressing any feeling, be it good or bad.

Remember

- A little help you give can go a long way.
- Never hesitate to help people.
- Practise selflessness. Don't expect anything in return of your help.
- Helpful people are considered dependable.
- People always remember how you helped them.

Figure out

A. Tick the correct answers.

1. The arrival of the telegraph made the family
   a. happy because it carried good news of their father.
   b. afraid because it carried bad news about their father.
2. When their mother cried, the four sisters?
   a. tried their best to console Mrs March.
   b. did not give Mrs March much importance.
3. During this miserable moment, each person
   a. was concerned about their own work.
   b. focused on how they could help Mrs March in some little way.
4. Jo could not be found anywhere because
   a. she had gone to the shop to sell her hair and earn money for her mother's journey.
   b. she had gone to the shops to buy a dress for herself.
5. Jo felt sad without her long hair but
   a. she felt she looked smarter with short hair.
   b. she was keen to get money for her mother in whichever way possible.

B. Write a diary entry about something you did that brought a smile on the face of your loved ones.

Relate

Tick the best options for these situations.

1. You hear your house help scolding her seven-year-old daughter because she has failed a Math test. What will you do?
   a. try to help your house help's daughter with her studies
   b. ignore the incident

2. There is a hostel for sight-impaired people near your home. It has many children too. What will you do?
   a. avoid going there as people with special needs make you uncomfortable ☐
   b. visit the hostel once a week to spend time with the children ☐
3. Your grandfather can hardly see but is keen to know the news of the day. What will you do?
   a. make sure you read the newspaper to him every day ☐
   b. ignore his condition and go about doing your own work ☐
4. There is no water in your apartment one day. So a tanker has been called for people to fill buckets and store water. Your elderly upstairs neighbour cannot carry buckets. What will you do?
   a. not bother how she gets her water because you have to fill buckets for your family ☐
   b. fill and carry her buckets to her home after you have filled for your family ☐

Act

Home Help Talk

1. Each student will write on a sheet of paper one chore that he or she has done the previous evening at home. At the bottom of the sheet, the student will write a few physical traits he or she has, such as long braid or big eyes
2. Once everyone has finished, all the sheets will be folded and put into a bowl and shaken up.
3. The bowl will be taken around the class and each student will pick out one sheet and first read the chore written on it and then the physical traits. Listening to the physical description, the rest of the class will try to guess who the writer is.
4. When the writer is correctly identified, then he or she can come up to the front of the class and give more details about the chore and how he or she felt while performing it.

Happiness Box

1. **May I Help You Badges**

Materials required

Felt paper, coloured cartridge paper, scissors, star and smiley face stickers, glitter glue, marker, safety pin

Method

1. Start by cutting a rectangle or a circle out of the felt and the cartridge sheet 3 x 3 inches.
2. Using glue, stick the paper on the felt. Write on the paper, MAY I HELP YOU?
3. Decorate the badge with a few stickers and then adorn with glitter glue.
4. Pin the badge to your shirt.

Wear the badges and offer help to people. It will be your kind deed for the day.

2. Recite this poem in class. Make three groups and each group can recite two lines of the poem while the entire class would recite the last line together.

If I Can Stop One Heart From Breaking

If I can stop one heart from breaking,
I shall not live in vain;
If I can ease one life the aching,
Or cool one pain,
Or help one fainting robin
Unto his nest again,
I shall not live in vain.

—Emily Dickinson

Teaching tips

- Ensure that students understand how even one small gesture or word can help a person who is sad.
- Stress on the fact that it is the duty of the strong and the able to help the weak.
- Inspire them to do at least one kind deed every day.

Goal 13: Climate Action

- Last five years were the hottest recorded on the Earth.
- Increasing greenhouse gas emissions cause climate change.
- Air pollution caused by vehicles and factories has increased the amount of carbon dioxide in the atmosphere.
- Weather patterns are changing, sea levels are rising, and weather events are becoming more extreme.

Extremely hot and dry weather caused bushfires in Australia!

The Arctic ice-caps are melting due to global warming.

The 3Rs

Recycle

- Make new things out of used or waste materials.
- Segregate waste into dry and wet. Keep paper, plastic, cardboard, metal and glass separate.

Reduce

- Use and consume less.
- Take measures to cut down waste.

Reuse

- Using an object again or differently than what it was intended for. For example, use old newspapers to wrap items and use old mugs as pen-stands.

Take A Stand!

Reduce your carbon footprint. Choose activities which reduce the amount of carbon dioxide released into the atmosphere.

Undertake a tree plantation drive in your neighbourhood. You can plant a trees on special occasions like birthdays.

Switch off lights, television, computers and other electrical appliances when not in use.

Walk, ride a bicycle, carpool or use public transport. Car exhaust contains harmful gases which pollute the air.

Avoid using plastic– it's an environmental disaster! Use cloth bags to shop and reusable bottles for drinking water.

Read and create awareness about use of renewable sources of energy. Adopt an energy-efficient lifestyle.

Project III : Greenhouse Effect

Write a project report on Greenhouse Effect. You can address the following questions in your project.

- What is the Greenhouse Effect?
- When was this term coined?
- What are the causes of the Greenhouse Effect?
- What are greenhouse gases?
- How does carbon dioxide play an important role in causing the Greenhouse Effect?
- What role do the automobiles play in causing the Greenhouse Effect?
- What are the problems caused by the Greenhouse Effect?
- How does the Greenhouse Effect cause global warming?
- How does Global Warming effect the global climate?
- What are the steps taken at the global level to reduce emissions causing the Greenhouse Effect?

....

....

....

....

....

....

....

....

....

....

....

....

....

....

....

Project IV : Famous Personalities

A. There were more people in history who are known for immense contribution to the world of medicine and nursing. Find out more about the names listed here, and write a project report on their contributions.

- Clara Barton, the Lady of the Battlefield
- Mary Todd Lincoln, the First Lady Nurse
- Mary Ezra Mahoney, the first African-American nurse
- Walt Whitman, the poet nurse
- Dr Dwarkanath Kotnis 'ke Dihua', the saviour in Sino-Japanese war in 1938

Clara Barton

Mary Todd Lincoln

Mary Ezra Mahoney

Walt Whitman

B. Write a paragraph about healthcare workers and how they risk their lives to save ours.

C. Draw or paste a picture of healthcare worker who inspires you.